MAY C

by Frankie Meredith

ǁSAMUEL FRENCHǁ

FOR AMATEUR PRODUCTION ENQUIRIES

UNITED KINGDOM AND WORLD
EXCLUDING NORTH AMERICA
licensing@concordtheatricals.co.uk
020-7054-7200

Each title is subject to availability from Concord Theatricals, depending upon country of performance.

The moral right of Frankie Meredith to be identified as author of this work has been asserted in accordance with Section 77 of the Copyright, Designs and Patents Act 1988.

USE OF COPYRIGHTED MUSIC

A licence issued by Concord Theatricals to perform this play does not include permission to use the incidental music specified in this publication. In the United Kingdom: Where the place of performance is already licensed by the PERFORMING RIGHT SOCIETY (PRS) a return of the music used must be made to them. If the place of performance is not so licensed then application should be made to PRS for Music (www.prsformusic.com.). A separate and additional licence from PHONOGRAPHIC PERFORMANCE LTD.(www. ppluk.com) may be needed whenever commercial recordings are used. Outside the United Kingdom: Please contact the appropriate music licensing authority in your territory for the rights to any incidental music.

USE OF COPYRIGHTED THIRD-PARTY MATERIALS

Licensees are solely responsible for obtaining formal written permission from copyright owners to use copyrighted third-party materials (e.g., artworks, logos) in the performance of this play and are strongly cautioned to do so. If no such permission is obtained by the licensee, then the licensee must use only original materials that the licensee owns and controls. Licensees are solely responsible and liable for clearances of all third-party copyrighted materials, and shall indemnify the copyright owners of the play(s) and their licensing agent, Concord Theatricals Ltd., against any costs, expenses, losses and liabilities arising from the use of such copyrighted third-party materials by licensees.

IMPORTANT BILLING AND CREDIT REQUIREMENTS

If you have obtained performance rights to this title, please refer to your licensing agreement for important billing and credit requirements.

CAST AND CREATIVE

FRANKIE MEREDITH | WRITER

Frankie is a Midlands-based playwright & theatre maker. Having gained a place on the Lyric Hammersmith Young Writers Programme she started writing short plays performed at various theatres around London. She wrote her first full length play TURKEY on the Soho Writers Lab which was produced at The Hope Theatre in 2017 to rave reviews & Off West End nominations. FINDING PETER a play for young audiences was taken up to Edinburgh & had two subsequent runs in London & her play 17 was produced at Vaults Festival by Wildcard Theatre & is being developed for television. Frankie is currently working on a folk musical about women from her area, along with Warwick Arts Centre, it will tour Coventry and Warwickshire in 2021. Her film CLEMENTINES recently won 'Best Short' at the British International Film Festival & she has recently written & directed a web-series BECOMING DANISH. Frankie was Paines Ploughs Playwright Fellow in 19-20 during which time she had some of her work translated into Catalan and performed in Barcelona.

YASMIN DAWES | LEIGH

Yasmin Dawes is a West Midlands-born actor and creative. She trained at Rose Bruford College and spent a semester as an acting major at Syracuse University in New York State. After graduating in 2019, she was cast in a Domino's commercial, though her work has mostly been within theatre. Most recently she played The Goddess in Futures Theatre's forum theatre tour UNDERWATER LOVE, and toured the north of the UK with Tmesis Theatre in their movement piece WICKED WOMEN. After a long year without her industry Yasmin is blessed to bounce back with Leigh in MAY QUEEN, an intersectional story dear to her heart.

BALISHA KARRA | DIRECTOR

Midlands-born Balisha Karra is a graduate from University of Birmingham. She has previously co-directed Meredith's play 17; meeting the writer prior as Trainee Director inside Paines Plough's Roundabout. For Balisha, directing MAY QUEEN felt like the perfect full circle. She feels MAY QUEEN speaks loudly to her younger self and hopes generations to come feel differently.

LYDIA DENNO | DESIGNER

Lydia is a visual artist. She studied Theatre Design at Nottingham Trent and graduated in 2007. She began her career as assistant designer on the award-winning Railway Children (National Railway Museum and King's Cross Theatre), and has gone on to develop an interdisciplinary practice which encompasses theatre, installation, illustration and even walking. She has worked for theatres such as York Theatre Royal, Nottingham Playhouse, The Lowry, Soho Theatre and Wembley Arena, as well as heritage sites around the UK and galleries internationally. Lydia's design work has been awarded an Eastern Eye Award and recently 'gained laurels' having been selected for the Tribeca Film Festival. She is excited by the stories that spaces and objects can tell, as well as the people that inhabit and use them. With Iraqi-British heritage, she is interested in cross-cultural storytelling and in particular stories that transcend physical and metaphysical borders. She is drawn towards under-represented stories and characters, interested in fleeting moments and gestures as performance, and enticed by what narratives lie in the detail.

RICHARD HOWELL | LIGHTING DESIGNER
Richard trained at Guildhall School of Music and Drama. Credits include: TARTUFFE, CORIOLANUS (RSC); THE WRITER (Almeida); ARISTOCRATS, PRIVACY (Donmar); ALL MY SONS, JEKYLL AND HYDE (Old Vic, London); PINTER 5 & 6, GLENGARRY GLEN ROSS, BAD JEWS, KILLER JOE (West End); I SEE YOU (Royal Court, Jerwood Theatre Upstairs); HOMECOMING, EAST IS EAST (Trafalgar Studios for Jamie Lloyd Company); CAT ON A HOT TIN ROOF, BREAKING THE CODE, A DOLL'S HOUSE, LITTLE SHOP OF HORRORS (Manchester Royal Exchange); LABYRINTH (Hampstead Theatre); THE COUNTRY WIFE (Chichester, Minerva); THE WILD PARTY (The Other Palace); FAUSTUS, THE GLASS MENAGERIE (Headlong, UK Tour); A MIDSUMMER NIGHT'S DREAM, THE WIZARD OF OZ, PLAYING FOR TIME (Sheffield Crucible); THE GRINNING MAN, THE CRUCIBLE, THE LIFE AND TIMES OF FANNY HILL (Bristol Old Vic); THE MADNESS OF GEORGE III (Nottingham Playhouse); PROJECT POLUNIN (Sadlers Wells); CABARET (Gothenburg Opera); BREAKING THE WAVES, FLIGHT (Scottish Opera); IL TRITTICO, MADAME BUTTERFLY, LA FANCIULLA (Opera Holland Park); MADAME BUTTERFLY (Danish National Opera).

KIERAN LUCAS | SOUND DESIGNER
Kieran is an award-nominated sound designer & theatre-maker. He is a founding member of Barrel Organ & associate artist at Coney. Credits include: THE FUTURE PROJECT (Streatham Space Project), FOUND SOUND (Coventry Creates/Coventry City of Culture), NOAH & THE PEACOCK (Nottingham Playhouse), ME FOR THE WORLD (Young Vic), THE RAGE OF NARCISSUS (Pleasance Islington), ANTIGONE (New Diorama), GASTRONOMIC (Shoreditch Town Hall/Norwich Theatre Royal), CONSPIRACY (Underbelly/New Diorama), POPS (HighTide Festival) COMPANION: MOON (Natural History Museum), HOW WE SAVE THE WORLD (Natural History Museum), THE EX-BOYFRIEND YARD SALE (CPT/Progress Festival), TBCTV (Somerset House), SQUARE GO (Paines Plough Roundabout/59E59), A GIRL IN SCHOOL UNIFORM (Walks Into A Bar) (New Diorama), MY NAME IS RACHEL CORRIE (Young Vic), BIG GUNS (The Yard), UNDER THE SKIN (St Paul's Cathedral).

KLOE DEAN | MOVEMENT DIRECTOR
Kloe is a Choreographer, Movement Director and Performing Artist from London, UK, specialising in hip-hop, funk and streetdance styles. Kloe is a Work Place artist at The Place, Kings Cross, Creative Director of all-female hip-hop dance company, Myself UK Dance, and has presented a range of dance theatre both nationally and internationally including Breakin Convention in London, Ladies Of Hip Hop in New York and The Sub Urban Danse Festival Copenhagen. Kloé has worked with a range of music artists including Little Simz, Cleo Sol and Rita Ora, as well as brands such as Jimmy Choo, Nike, Marks & Spencer's and George at ASDA.

KALEYA BAXE | ASSISTANT DIRECTOR
Kaleya Baxe is a writer, director and facilitator whose work is driven by her passion for representation, inclusion and a collaborative process. As well as working on outreach and youth projects with the Young Vic, Kiln, Arcola Theatre and several drama schools, her work often shines a light on important subjects (PATRICIA GETS READY (FOR A DATE WITH THE MAN THAT USED TO HIT HER)) and has toured schools, youth settings and pupil referral units (WRITTEN, Little Fish Theatre). As an assistant she has worked with acclaimed writers such as Chinonyerem Odimba (Artistic Director, Tiata Fahodzi) and Mike Bartlett (DOCTOR FOSTER, LIFE). Kaleya trained at the Royal Central School of Speech and Drama on the Drama, Applied Theatre and Education course. Her work as a director includes; 786 by Ric Renton (Paines Plough R&D, LAMDA), PATRICIA GETS READY (FOR A DATE WITH THE MAN THAT USED TO HIT HER) by Martha Watson Allpress (Pleasance, VAULT Festival Show of the Week Award Winner) and WRITTEN by Alex Cooke (Little Fish Theatre, Schools and Youth Settings Tour).

WABRIYA KING | DRAMATHERAPIST
Wabriya graduated as an actress from The Oxford School of Drama in 2012. After several years working as an actress in a variety of roles, she decided to take her career in a different direction and graduated from the University of Roehampton with an MA in Dramatherapy in 2019. Since qualifying, she has worked alongside: ROMEO & JULIET – Shakespeare's Globe, THE DEATH OF A BLACK MAN – Hampstead Theatre, SEVEN METHODS OF KILLING KYLIE JENNER – The Royal Court, SHUCK N JIVE – Soho Theatre, 846 Live – Theatre Royal Stratford East, TYPICAL – Soho Theatre, THE HIGH TABLE – Bush Theatre. She believes that the arts have a responsibility to its performers to support their mental health wellbeing. This is clearly a shared belief as her work is gaining momentum within the sector.

AIME NEEME | COMPANY STAGE MANAGER
Aime is a LAMDA trained freelance theatre director and stage manager.

Past credits include; PARAKEET (Boundless), HARD FEELINGS, THE HOTEL PLAYS, A LIE OF THE MIND (Defibrillator Theatre), DENNIS OF PENGE (Ovalhouse).

BENJAMIN SMITH | TECHNICAL STAGE MANAGER
Benjamin graduated from the Stage Management and Technical Theatre course at the Royal Welsh College of Music and Drama in 2018. Since leaving he has had a varied work career, Sound Designing, Re-Lighting, as well as both Technical and Company Stage Management. Previous work includes: JANE EYRE (Blackeyed Theatre), ANIMAL FARM (Pegasus Theatre), ANNA KARENINA (Pegasus Theatre), UNFORTUNATE (Fat Rascal Theatre), VULVARINE (Fat Rascal Theatre), WORD GET'S AROUND (RCT Theatre), MEMORY OF WATER (ALRA North), 2023 (Illumine Theatre Company).

PHILIP THACKRAY | TECHNICAL STAGE MANAGER
Philip Thackray is one of this technical stage managers for this year's Roundabout tour, having worked previously on the 2019 Roundabout tour and a large background in fringe theatre and outdoor events. Phil currently works as freelance theatre and live event technician having worked often with Theatr Clywd on a number of their productions and with T-bats for their outdoor events. Credits-Technical Crew ROUNDABOUT TOUR - 2019. Senior Build Crew and Senior Event Supervisor GUNG HO tour 2018, 2019. Stage Technician 2018 HANSEL & GRETEL: FAIRYTALE DETECTIVES – Theatr Clywd.

Paines Plough

Paines Plough are a touring theatre company dedicated to new writing; we find, develop and empower writers across the country and share their explosive new stories with audiences all over the UK and beyond.

"The lifeblood of the UK's theatre ecosystem." *The Guardian*

Since 1974 Paines Plough has worked with over 300 outstanding British playwrights including James Graham, Sarah Kane, Dennis Kelly, Mike Bartlett, Sam Steiner, Elinor Cook, Vinay Patel, Zia Ahmed and Kae Tempest.

Our plays are nationally identified and locally heard. We tour to over 40 places a year and are committed to bringing work to communities who might not otherwise have the opportunity to experience much new writing or theatre. We reach over 30,000 people annually from Cornwall to the Orkney Islands, in village halls and in our own pop-up theatre Roundabout; a state of the art, in the round auditorium which travels the length and breadth of the country.

"That noble company Paines Plough, de facto national theatre of new writing." *Daily Telegraph*

Furthering our reach beyond theatre walls our audio app COME TO WHERE I'M FROM hosts 180 original mini plays about home and our digital projects connect with audiences via WhatsApp, phone, email and even by post.

Wherever you are, you can experience a Paines Plough Production.

"I think some theatre just saved my life." @kate_clement on Twitter

Paines Plough Limited is a company limited by guarantee and a registered charity.
Registered Company no: 1165130
Registered Charity no: 267523
Paines Plough, 2nd Floor, 10 Leake Street, London SE1 7NN

+ 44 (0) 20 7240 4533
office@painesplough.com
www.painesplough.com
Follow @PainesPlough on Twitter

Follow @painesplough on Instagram
Like Paines Plough at facebook.com/PainesPloughHQ
Donate to Paines Plough at justgiving.com/PainesPlough

Paines Plough ROUNDABOUT

"A beautifully designed masterpiece in engineering." *The Stage*

ROUNDABOUT is Paines Plough's beautiful portable in-the-round theatre. It's a completely self-contained 168-seat auditorium that flat packs into a single lorry and pops up anywhere from theatres to school halls, sports centres, warehouses, car parks and fields.

We built ROUNDABOUT to tour to places that don't have theatres. ROUNDABOUT travels the length and breadth of the UK bringing the nation's best playwrights and a thrilling theatrical experience to audiences everywhere.

Over the last six years ROUNDABOUT has hosted over 2,000 hours of entertainment for more than 100,000 people in places ranging from a churchyard in Salford to Margate seafront.

ROUNDABOUT was designed by Lucy Osborne and Emma Chapman at Studio Three Sixty in collaboration with Charcoalblue and Howard Eaton.

WINNER of Theatre Building of the Year at The Stage Awards 2014.

"ROUNDABOUT venue wins most beautiful interior venue by far @edfringe." @ChaoticKirsty on Twitter

"ROUNDABOUT is a beautiful, magical space. Hidden tech make it Turkish-bath-tranquil but with circus-tent-cheek. Aces." @evenicol on Twitter

ROUNDABOUT was made possible thanks to the belief and generous support of the following Trusts and individuals and all who named a seat in Roundabout. We thank them all.

TRUSTS AND FOUNDATIONS	CORPORATE
Andrew Lloyd Webber Foundation	Universal Consolidated Group
Paul Hamlyn Foundation	Howard Eaton Lighting Ltd
Garfield Weston Foundation	Charcoalblue
J Paul Getty Jnr Charitable Trust	Avolites Ltd
John Ellerman Foundation	Factory Settings
	Total Solutions

Roundabout is supported by the Theatres Trust in 2021.

Pop your name on a seat and help us pop-up around the UK: https://www.justgiving.com/fundraising/roundaboutauditorium

Theatres Trust

Supported using public funding by

**ARTS COUNCIL
ENGLAND**

The Belgrade Theatre Coventry

Together, with the diverse communities across Coventry and the region, we aim to enrich and fundamentally change people's lives for the better through theatre.

In our landmark building, across the region, the UK and online, we will use theatre to entertain, inspire, share the city's stories, uncover hidden histories and unleash the creativity in our communities.

The Belgrade is the largest professional theatre in Coventry and so we act as both the city and region's commercial and producing theatre. We are also highly respected for our ground-breaking community and education initiatives. Hamish Glen is the current Artistic Director and Chief Executive.

The Belgrade is a registered charity and receives revenue funding from Coventry City Council and Arts Council England as well as project funding from these and other government sources.

The Belgrade played a key role in securing Coventry as UK City of Culture 2021 and in 2019 we appointed Corey Campbell, Balisha Karra and Justine Themen as Co-Artistic Directors, with a remit to programme and direct the Theatre's produced work for UK City of Culture 2021.

Senior Management Team

Hamish Glen
CHIEF EXECUTIVE & ARTISTIC DIRECTOR
Joanna Reid
EXECUTIVE DIRECTOR
Corey Campbell
2021 CO-ARTISTIC DIRECTOR
Balisha Karra
2021 CO-ARTISTIC DIRECTOR
Justine Themen
2021 CO-ARTISTIC DIRECTOR
Sâmir Bhamra
2021 SENIOR PRODUCER
Vera Ding
GENERAL MANAGER
Adrian Sweeney
DIRECTOR OF PRODUCTION
Richard Hope-Jones
GENERAL MANAGER – BPS
Nicola Young
DIRECTOR OF COMMUNICATIONS
Ray Clenshaw
COMMUNICATIONS MANAGER
Helen Hotchkiss
HEAD OF DEVELOPMENT
Paul Newsome
FINANCIAL CONTROLLER

MAY QUEEN was produced by Roundabout 2021: A Paines Plough and Belgrade Theatre Coventry Production, part of Coventry City of Culture 2021, on 29 July, 2021 and then toured the UK. The cast and creative team were as follows:

LEIGH . . . . .Yasmin Dawes

Director	Balisha Karra
Designer	Lydia Denno
Lighting Designer	Richard Howell
Sound Designer	Kieran Lucas
Associate Sound Designer	Bella Kear
Movement Director	Kloe Dean
Assistant Director	Kaleya Baxe
Dramaturg	Sarah Dickenson
Dramatherapist	Wabriya King
Casting Director	Jacob Sparrow
Costume Supervisor	Rhiannon Hawthorn
Movement Support	Esme Benjamin
Lighting Programmer	Sam Ohlsson
Company Stage Manager	Aime Neeme
Technical Stage Managers	Benjamin Smith, Philip Thackray
Rehearsal Stage Manager	Ella Stewart
Stage Management Support	Ruth Porter

With Thanks To:	V&A Productions
	Abbie Morgan

CHARACTERS

LEIGH – sixteen

AUTHOR'S NOTES

regular when Leigh is talking to us

italics when she's in a convo chattin to someone else

> *indent italics when it IS someone else.*

space indicates length of pause

/ cut off

... trail off.

*** change of scene/location/vibe

~~struck text~~ spoken or implied, your choice.

&

This is very much a Coventry play, please keep all references and setting in Cov. Try to find an actor from this area or at least one that can do the accent.

FOR ALL THE TEENAGE GIRLS
(and those of us who have been and those of us who will).

(**LEIGH** *walks to the edge of the stage.*)

(*A peach dress.*)

(*A ritual.*)

Godiva, Godiva will you bury them?

Godiva, Godiva will you bury him?

A sign of hope in peaceless times

A sign of hope in peaceless times

A shining light amongst the darkest nights

A shining light amongst the darkest nights

One day the tide is turning

And nothing will be left for them

Godiva will you bury them?

Godiva will you ride again?

And when your silent rage will come

No man will be the chosen one

Godiva, Godiva will come

Godiva, Godiva will come

Godiva will you finish him?

Godiva, Godiva will come

Alright?

I'm Leigh. The *May Queen.*

Although you probs seen the posters,

that's why you're here?

thanks for coming.

thankyouthankyouthankyou.

And don't worry.

I'm not gonna keep talking in rhymes like that.

Just a bit of theatrics to pull you in like.

you alright?

alright?

I like your top.

you're meana say 'i like your dress'.

thank you.

although it ended up soaked in blood.

proper covered,

goes everywhere dunt it?

and mum struggled get the stains out.

she was piiiiissed off.

now you wanna know how it gets soaked in blood right?

not mine.

chill out.

I'll tell ya.

THIS IS THE STORY ABOUT...

THIS IS A STORY OF...

THIS

IS

MAY QUEEN...

***

After the absolute shitstorm that has bin the last couple
of years my area – Coventry...

> *(Responds to any audience acknowledgment.*
> *encourage it.)*

...wanted to celebrate with a folk-festival.

To honour All-Things-English

whatthefuuuck?

why does it feel so weird when we do anything,

what's that word?

...*patriotic.*

Like the Americans love a flag,

they all have um in their front gardens

and on hats n things, they don't give a shit.

and the Portuguese!

The Portuguese cafe down our road is litch covered in
their flags.

But as soon as anyone puts a St George's up it's like,

urgh...

So for this England Festival they want things like,

May-pole,

Morris dancin,

May Queen.

I'd never even heard of a May Queen before.

Which basically meant emailing someone at the council (if you were a girl in a CV postcode between the ages of fifteen to seventeen) and they was gonna invite you for an interview and see if you were Queen material.

It became this massive thing at school like,

everyone wanted to do it.

I think after being cooped up for a coupla years we was all just buzzing to put on a dress.

Peeps were chattin about it,

talking in class about it,

dm'in about it.

we had GCSEs coming up but this is all anyone would speak about.

it became like, **proper important.**

So when I went home and asked my mum if i could put my name in, she gave me this cute smile, and told me 'she already had'.

my mums LOVES shit like this. like proper loves it. she's a *girls* girls.

good job she's got three of us.

girls

...apparently all the way up until I was born they thought I was gonna be a boy.

True story.

They had a name picked out.

She'd bought loadsa shit from like Next or somewhere,

that was blue,

all of it was blue.

My dad was buzzing his tits off.

This woman at mum's work had tied one of her rings to a piece of string

and held it over the bump.

it went in a circle

so they said i would be a boy.

Then at the scan, I had my legs crossed so the lady doing it said she couldn't really tell but I think it's a boy,

cheers love,

any way... I wasn't.

So when I came, after seventy-three hours, my dad stormed out. Just like, walked straight out of the birthing room. Punched a wall, bought a Lucozade from the vending machine, came back in.

And said.

'we're still calling it Ashleigh'

he left three weeks later, for good.

And mum hasn't called me Ashleigh since, but Leigh, always Leigh.

She knows how to pick um my mum.

Which is weird coz she's really, what's it...perceptive?

but when it comes to men it's like she's had a fuckin lobotomy.

when we watched the news, about a body that's been found or summin, she's all

'oh *he* did it, look at his eyes'

or she'd like pick someone out from the background and be like

'them, it's them. look at their eyes'.

she's right ya know.

most of the time.

thing is

all her boyfriends

have those crazy fuckin eyes.

But, she does sweet stuff like put me up for the May Queen.

So when we got the email telling us i was being invited for an interview

oh my days, she went off it.

she was dancing round the kitchen

with me and my sisters, the baby.

she even shared her box of wine wiv us.

which tastes like absolute shit but we was just happy to be having a drink.

my mum, gets up, on a chair,

holds up her glass

my older sister who's vaping out the window

(coz we dunt know what it does to the little ones yet)

rolls her eyes,

as mum starts:

(As mum, tipsy.)

Here's to my baby

my middley

my Leigh

she is the one, who is so pretteeey,

muuum

i knew she would do it

nuffin else to it

mum you can't rhyme two 'its'.

shhh it's my speech

and just as she drew her breath

for another verse of this *beautiful* poetry,

a bird fuckin flies IN the window that ma sister's sittin at,

she loses everything and jumps down,

screaming.

my little sister joins in

coz my big sister shit her up

and the baby starts crying

coz she don't wanna be left out.

my mum calm as anything stays on her chair

smiling

saying

> *it's your grandad*
>
> *don't worry*
>
> *y'alright dad?*
>
> *it's your grandad.*

she's pissed so she ent gonna do nuffin.

So I grab a box of wheat-bix

(weetabix if you don't shop at Aldi)

and sort of gently, but with force, smack this bird out our kitchen.

my sister slams the window shut

but the cocky shit

the cocky shit.

it comes back

and sits on the window ledge

and stares at us.

mum starts crying

and i think she's gonna do another poem about this bird.

but instead she drains the box of wine and goes into the lounge to watch the chase.

i go upstairs and google

'what does it mean when a bird flies in your window'

shouldn't have done that,

coz i get about 21,000,000 results of it being a

bad omen.

***

You ever been to the council offices in Cov?

i know i know you think Cov's a shithole

but the offices?

they're like one of the only thing that survived them bombs

and from the outside,

the building,

it's fit.

proper old and beaut.

really tall and this sort of deep reddy brown.

and you can see the cathedral spires out the back.

it feels like the sorta place a queen comes ya know?

and standing there,

waiting for: Mark,

Chief Cultural Officer Mark,

I'm

looking at all the engravings n that

and

i feel a bit proud of coming from Cov

which hasn't happened before, ever.

it's got statues of old nuns or summin

and men that look a bit like the pope

but it's also got an elephant,

right above the door

and i **love** elephants.

and there's like tigers

and flowers

and

looks sick, actually,

looks like a palace or /

    / Ashleigh?

?

    Ashleigh Jackson?

it's Leigh.

    Mark Timms, CCO.

oh, y'alright?

and Mark living up to his name,

looking like he wears nuffin but Marks and Sparks

says he

    recognised you from my picture

and asked me to follow him.

making our way through the

yeh

pretty grimey corridors

(it ent posh inside)

he asks if I would like a

    tea or coffee?

i said no thanks but i'd love a squash

and instantly regretted it.

who asks for a squash?

He leads me into this stuffy little room and starts to talk all about how much he loved Coventry and how fun this May Day was gonna be...

so what we thought'd make this day really pop, yeah pop. is like a couple of characters that we could dot around the place. just to make it interesting. so people can really get a feel for the history of the city you know

right

but we didn't wanna use actors, we wanted real local people.

ok

thought it'd feel more authentic.

and I'm thinking 'mate I'm just here for the dress'

He then goes on to tell me:

we want to have a May Queen to hark back to the days of old, so it feels more pagan – you know pagan? That's the vibe we're going for.

this guy has never said 'vibe' before in his life.

And we'll have the May Queen parade through the city and end up at Coffa's Tree, which is the, place where Coventry began. As a sort of ritual, a nod to our roots.

and what happens at the tree?

well i did wanna go all out and sacrifice a virgin, but health and safety you know...

what?

uhh,

the word virgin just sort of hangs in the air and i see the blind panic in his face that he's just tried to make a joke about virgins and death and

a bit of banter

never mind

sorry?

So we thought we'd make it a competition. and you won. Congratulations.

I've got it?

I, I thought this was an interview?

we've met all our candidates, and out of everyone i think you look most, suitable.

ok?

Further information will be sent in but if you would like to choose an appropriate dress for the occasion we'll happily donate the sum of forty pounds, *mind the role is of May Queen, therefore we require it to be of a pastel colour and please keep in mind 'pure, virtuous and maidenly' when making your purchase.*

Thanks Leigh, good to meet you.

On the way out I see another girl waiting in the foyer who's wearing a skin coloured body stocking.

Obv she's going for the role of Godiva.

I would have gone for that but I'm not wearing no body stocking

and I sure as hell ain't going near no horse.

Sparks says he *really* looks forward to seeing you in my dress,

and guides me out the room with his hand on my

arse.

my lower back.

my back.

outside.

> *(Breath.)*

i voice-note Sienna,

alright babe. kneeldownforyourqueen. guess who just fuckin got it??? basically wasn't even an interview, he just said i looked the part. and gave it to me. AND said i've got forty quid to spend on a dress. so...thank you Sparks hun. gonna go home.

i voice note mum.

hi muuum. I GOT IT! gonna go round Sienna's, tell you about it later. love you.

***

I don't go to either of these places.

I go to Callum's.

Coz Callum has got the weed.

and I need something to calm – me – down.

> *(Iiiiinhaaaaales. Exhaaaaaales.)*

***

Calms isn't my boyfriend.

he's a friend sort of,

that's a boy

and we fuck.

but most of the time.

i just sit on his sofa and smoke

and wait for them to finish playing shooting games.

there's a group of us, that hang out together

since little school.

well

they hang out

and we, the girls, any girls, just sort of

hang *around* them.

waiting.

not really waiting for anything,

their attention

maybe.

even from really little

in the playground,

I'd wait for them to ask me to play with them.

Or if we was playing something like

Pirates

i'd just be waiting *eternally* to get captured

or if we was playing football

I'd just be waiting for them to pass me the ball.

and waiting for them outside the shop

and waiting for them to dm

and waiting for their likes

and waiting for them to finish their game so i can tell
them that

i'm gonna be the May Queen

    (Inhale, exhale.) you lot still chattin about that?

yeah but i got it, i won.

    (Inhale, exhale.) what does it mean?

it's like a tradition innit? from the old days. from pagan times.

    (Inhale, exhale.) sound.

they're giving me forty quid for it so it's basically paid.

    yeh?

yeh.

    cool.

obviously he doesn't get it

which is fine

but i thought he might say a well done or summin.

he says nothing after that.

and we have the kind of sex where I feel like he doesn't know if it's my body or the xbox controller.

and i walk home.

it's like two minutes.

out of Budbrooke

onto Milverton lane

keep going till

      (Boyonabike.)

   oiiiiiiii

keep going till I get to Hillmorton Road

oiiii pretty girl

keep going.

i'm talking to you

like just keep going straight.

what ya being rude for?

then at the junction cross over

is alright, i could watch you walk all night.

onto lapworth road

sket

and right into Moon crescent.

Cute right?

moon crescent.

we used to love it when we was little.

It's after ten so mum's out of it.

on the sofa.

when she's on a day shift she can blackout by nine pm

when she's on a night shift she can blackout by nine am.

she's very good at timings.

i sit down

finish her vodka

and tell her sleeping body how my interview went.

On the TV there are naked people standing behind screens

and a man picking which one he wants to date

and it scares me

it fucking scares me.

getting old.

i stare at their skin and their

saggy bits.

can't stop myself

my sister leans in the doorway

    what ye watching this for?
it was just on.
    sick ent it?
yeah
    why would anyone wanna do that? on tv?
dunno.
    why would anyone wanna watch that?
dunno
i got may queen
    yeh mum said
    / i'm going to bed.
night
    you gonna keep watching this shit?
nah.

I stay up till three watching back to back episodes.

I can't take our eyes off these ancient

bits.

it's not the elbows I'm looking at

I'm staring at these

boobs

and

bums

and

vagina.

I lie next to mum and google

Coffa's Tree

turns out it *is* a thing.

and i go into a hole.

then i dig my way into

virgin sacrifice.

but nothing links the two

except

Sparks.

i google Mark Timms.

i don't find much except somethin called a LinkedIn
profile

which is very dull

and then his instagram

where i can see

he has a girlfriend called Molly

and a dog called Tilly.

Or the other way around.

***

The next day

Sienna's offered to help me pick my dress.

she's good like that,

always there for me and my fashion choices

which she saaaays

i have a tendency to

   not get quuiiite right

Now if this was some old school film we'd be silky montaging in a load of different outfits.

but you're in a tent in Cov and it's 2021

so we do all our picking online.

pure

virtuous

maidenly

we decide that it means I need to look like I might have sex with you, but that I'd back out at the last minute then go milk a cow or summin.

which is a lot of layers

to get off ASOS.

We've narrowed it down to three

a short at the front, long at the back lilac.

a ruffly peach with spaghetti straps.

sky blue with boobs galore.

Sienna says she's gonna go and decide while she sits on
the loo

and i hear him coming before i see him.

(The sound of football boots.)

clack

clack

clack clack

clackclackclack

clack

clack clack

clack clack clack clack clack

    alright.

alright.

clack clack

clack clack

clack

clack clack.

Sienna's brother ~~Kofi~~, but we call him Klack.

He's four years older than us

and everyone thought he was gonna be some football
star

but he hurt his knee and now just plays semi pro.

he never takes his boots off.

like if he takes um off he's admitting that he's failed.

and what else has he got?

he just sort of like, clacks, around.

We used to practice kissing when I was ten

We used to practice a lot of stuff when i was eleven.

I've never told Sienna.

She'd go ape shit.

   ok it's definitely this one.

Sienna announces.

my decision made for me.

but i ping the peach one over to sparks,

for his *approval*

But really it's just so i can get the forty quid quick.

***

I don't hear from him for a long time

like long enough that i think did i make the whole thing up?

but in April i get forty quid in my account,

and a short email telling me a time and a place to meet him

on the day.

may day.

and there's a map attached

on a pdf

showing hillmorton

and budbrooke

and moon crescent

and the wood

and the trees,

and all the places I've ever known

but most importantly

coffa's tree

or where mark thinks his tree might be.

April warms everything up,

it's like everything been dead for a bit and the heat is
bringing us all back to life.

School's going mad about GCSEs

i ent even picked a college course yet

and it just keeps getting hotter.

which means,

I spend more time with Calm coz he supplies the weed,

and more time drinking,

coz the heat makes you thirsty...

and we spend more time just

laying

on whatever bit of grass we can find

***

The evening before.

a day that's been too hot to play computer games,

there's a few of us

at the park

right on the edge of the wood.

no one's talking much

just listening

or smoking

or, waiting.

sienna's posted a tiktok that's got 6,000 views already

so she's gone into shock.

and

i can't stop thinking about the fuckin tree.

i ask Callum if he wants to go and find it with me.

what tree you chattin about?

Coffa's Tree.

who da fuck is Coffa?

The guy that invented Cov

(Tuts, or summin.) Never heard of him.

so d'ya wanna come up there with me or not? I just wanna at least see it before. so i know where to go.

ask Jay. he's into history n shit like that.

(Turns to Jay.)

so the funny thing about Jay is

we used to be really tight

super close

we've even had baths together

when we was little.

his mum and my mum are mates,

n that's just what you do innit

bathe your kids together.

i used to make him sit there in silence,

so i could hear what the mums said.

> *i just can't get her to tell the truth*
>
> *i've had to tell three people this week that i'm not pregnant*
>
> *do i look pregnant to you???*
>
> *thank you.*
>
> *it's embarrassing.*
>
> *last month she told some kid at school that she got an adder for her birthday*
>
> *an adder*
>
> *a fuckin snake Stace,*
>
> *had her teacher take me aside and ask,*
>
> *like i was in some sort of trouble*
>
> *this kid had told his parents.*
>
> *but she doesn't care*
>
> *she just says it.*
>
> *says what she wants.*
>
> *i don't lie*
>
> *i'm a very honest person.*

maybe gets it from her dad?

speaking of dads...

has you know who been round recently?

maaan, i'll tell ya what,

if he was my baby's dad i'd wanna chop his dick off.

the next day at school i told everyone that Jay's mum tried to chop his dad's dick off. careful what you say around your kids.

and then at secondary school he became best mates with Callum

and we've stayed just as silent ever since.

but now, I'm all...

you wanna come?

n he's all

   alright.

n up the woods we're just walking about tryna find this tree

which could look like any other tree

and there are a shit load of um

but i thought maybe there'd be a sign or summin.

   (She can't stop looking at jay.)

Jay isn't talking

but he lights a joint and holds it out for me.

and he sorta smiles

and it reminds me of when we was seven.

the smile

not the spliff ;)

You heard about this tree before then?

    nah

oh. Callum said you liked learning about history?

    s'alright. doing about the war in GCSE. i like that.

yeh i do geography.

    i know.

n then silence.

and i can't fuckin deal with silence can i.

so…

remember when we used to have baths together?

    yeh sorta.

and we walk in this silence

our silence

till

we find the tree

the one we think it could be.

oldest looking

the one with saggy bits

and knots in the wood

and it looks

magnificent.

on people those things ain't good.

but on this tree,

Coffa's tree,

it's one of the most beautiful things I've ever seen.

its branches reaching up and coming back down in to the earth

the trunk not even visible coz branches have twisted around it

and

Jay sits at the base,

unaffected,

rolls a joint.

and i wonder what it's like to not think as much.

i sit next to him for a bit

we start to kiss under it for a bit

and we become...the greatest love story thats ever been told!

jokes,

the night before I'm queen.

i wake up in his bed.

***

(Alarm.

Grooooooan

Grooooooooans.

    Alarm.

    Looks down at Jay.)

shit.

***

    (Boyonabike.)

  oiiiiiiii

queen

  oiiii pretty girl

the may queen

  i'm talking to you

not feeling very regal right now

  what ya being rude for?

luckily Jay lives just round the corner so...

  is alright, i could watch you walk all morning

  sket

***

Home and
I can hear them downstairs having breakfast together.
they heard the door slam,
the questions don't come

but they will.

in the bath i've learnt

If you keep your head under water – you don't feel hungover.

so

I keep my head under water.

for ages

and

ages and ages and ages.

(Gasp.)

A queen must prepare

everything i wash with smells fruity.

it all makes me feel a little bit, nauseous.

why do they want us to smell like fruit?

Stepping out i wrap my

coconut

papaya

citrus

strawberry

body

in a towel and pad to my bedroom.

Mum's made pancakes,

I say *made,* she bought them in a packet and heats um up in the microwave coz the toaster broke but

it's the effort that counts, right?

she's hung my dress up on my door,

she's ironed it.

it makes me wanna cry.

that's nice of her.

i must remember to thank her.

Downstairs and

everyone beams at me.

they don't ask me any questions about where I've been,
not one.

Big sis gets out a bottle from the fridge.

orange juice and champagne already mixed

feels posh.

feels like a wedding.

my wedding

she pops it.

i know if i just push through this first glass,

     (She downs it.)

She offers to do my make up.

why you being so nice?

we copy someone off youtube.

she does a really good job, actually.

my hair's poppin

my skin glows

and despite,

last night,

i think i look pure and virtuous and maidenly.

all those words Sparks asked for.

i take one more swig of the bottle

and another and another.

i look great!

kiss the baby goodbye

who i shit you not, looks at me more adoringly than she
normally does

i think it's the falsies,

making my eyes look HUGE,

but kinda itchy.

and tell um all i'll see um later.

i'll wave to them,

when I'm up there,

the peasants.

***

Leaving the house it feels hot.

Like hot hot.

Holiday hot.

I've only been to Mallorca.

We went one August to visit a friend of mum's who
lived there.

all of us in this tiny little apartment that smelt like
bleach

still the best week of my life though.

one day i spent eleven hours in the pool.

Anyway it's that kinda hot here.

And it's <u>May</u>.

what's that about?

People talk about it being global warming.

Which sucks coz; Cheers Brian for fuckin up the planet!

But I kinda like the heat. Don't tell anyone.

So Cov's looking like England has just won the world cup.

St George's everywhere.

There's a different vibe

like a party vibe

you can feel it

pulsing.

Barriers are being put up,

which will keep the crowds back,

from me.

And the sun is glinting off the tents

and the marquees

and the stalls that are all set up

in my kingdom.

workers busying away to get ready for the day.

People are starting to look,

I guess the dress is a lil extra.

but they're looking in a good way.

a really good way, i think.

i see him, in his linen suit, waving

he looks excited. that's sweet.

he's even got a flower tucked behind his ear.

i wave back.

n he sort of, lurches over,

> *that dress is just even better on isn't it?*

thanks

> *and you, you're glowing. your skin is just so, bright.*
> *it looks, almost...wet?*

it's dewy.

but actually it's sweat.

is there any water?

> *uhhhh. ummmm. we're trying not to do plastic, so,*
> *i'm not sure where the bottles are. uhhh, let me find*
> *out.*

s'alright, i'll just go to the offie.

> *brill. fab. super helpful, thanks Ashleigh.*

The place hasn't changed since I was a little kid.

I'd always go in to buy my mum bits she needed,

I'd beg her to let me go to the shop,

like it was the most exciting thing in the world.

some sort of adventure.

how small your world is when you're a kid.

and the guy was always nice to me behind the counter,

cute to me coz i was little,

letting the five p go if I was a bit short and wanted a
crunchie or summin.

But today,

i dunno if it's coz of the buzzy air or what

or coz my dress looks banging, buuuut

as i'm choosing which brightly coloured can has got enough shit in it to give me a kick,

i can feel his eyes boring into the back of me

and I turn around and he's

looking me up

and down

and up

and down,

and

part of me wants to shout

I'M A KID YOU SHOULD STILL BE GIVING ME FIVE P OFF A CRUNCHIE.

but the other part feels like, yeh, this is how,

this is how they'll all be looking at me today.

this is how they'll all look at me now.

so drink it in.

i put my can on the counter

he clears his throat.

go on,

i think.

praise your queen.

> *cough* your mum know you're out dressed like this?

I'm May Queen today, it's for the parade.

*That's a lot of flesh for the May Queen. I wouldn't be
happy if my daughter wore a dress like that.*

***

B

Back

Back outside the float has arrived.

Mark stood next to it,

arm outstretched like a kid, well proud of himself.

how brill is this.

what is it?

it's an elephant. see, look at the trunk.

but it's blinding me,

an yeah, it's an elephant, i guess.

but it's made up of old recycled car parts,

so it's all silver and metal.

and the sun is bouncing off it so bright that you can't
really look directly at it.

wow.

the little kids arrive. with their mums.

so cute.

and a dad omg.

he looks awkward af and definitely doesn't wanna be
here.

i wonder where her mum is.

the little girls look up at me like i am a princess or
something.

it's nice.

they're shown the float and where they should stand.

there are two other girls who are like twelve, thirteenish.

they come and hang around next to me.

my attendants.

    they tell me i'm pretty

i tell them they're pretty

    they tell me my dress is nice

i tell them their dresses are nice.

    they hunch over their phones the whole time.

giggling.

tucking their hair behind their ears, tilting their heads to the side and getting ready for the attention.

the dad of the little girl is looking at us,

he's trying not to.

i smile at him so he knows i caught it

but it makes him look longer,

feel more confident in his gaze.

his little girl's ponytail has come out

but he doesn't notice.

far too busy /

/ mum's arrived.

she's bought a picnic chair and is sitting behind a barrier.

she waves at me.

i wave back.

she marks out the territory for the others.

my sisters aren't there yet

but

oh god

she's with Jay's mum.

of course she is.

i message Callum a pic of me

he sends this face back

> (*Sticks her tongue out and winks.*)

i dm jay a pic of me.

he sends nothing back.

i take a cider from this

massive stack.

no one notices.

swig.

There's a hog, roasting.

turning.

warming up.

its skin crackling and blistering.

the smell makes me feel hungry and sick at the same
time.

swig.

a group of men are gathered around the poor pig,

talking about it.

pointing bits out,

bits that taste the nicest.

i feel sorry for it.

and i vow to be a vegetarian.

swig.

little kids need the loo

must be the excitement coz,

same babe,

but their mums take them.

the mums are wearing pastel as well,

like they're involved.

> *no one cares about you now love, you had your chance* – i think.

swig.

stash.

mark comes over rubbing his hands

> *feeling ready?*

he leaps up onto the float in a way i didn't think over thirties could

and reaches his hand out to help me up.

and I see my throne,

glistening,

shimmering in the heat.

the firemen are behind us.

on their own float

they ask me to

   do my best royal wave

(i do)

one says he

   wants more than a wave,

i stop

   that's not how a queen behaves

                                    ***

From up here,

you can see how many people have arrived

looks like

hundreds

maybe even thousands.

a band starts up

steel pans?

don't get me wrong

i love a steel pan,

but

they're not english.

i say to Mark.

he looks at me, confused.

    remember to keep smiling and waving
    keep smiling and waving.

We start our steady roll /

i see peeps from

primary school

secondary school

kids from my street

aunties

that aren't aunties but we call, aunty.

sienna and her brother are there,

with their mum and Dad

kids with their mums and

Dads and

i wonder if any of these are my dad?

i try and catch eyes with any men

eyes that might look a bit like mine,

i don't remember anything about my dad.

not one thing.

ent even seen a picture.

i used to pretend he was really Orlando Bloom.

i'd tell the kids at school and some actually believed
me. i even started to believe it myself.

i'd spend hours googling him and looking at paparazzi
pictures of him coming out of shops or

getting in cars and try and find some sort of...
resemblance.

never could.

Or-Lan-Do

good name int it?

no one round here would ever be called a name like
that.

Guys round here are called

Jay.

and

Kofi

and

Mark

and Coffa.

and

my eyes are now on

Callum

he's there,
perched on a wall at the back with a mate.
i smile and wave
and smile and wave
and smile

he's not even looking up

look up – i beg

look

up.

but next to him

jay looks up,

the men from the hog roast

now gazing at me,

which bits of me they'd think would taste the nicest,

and,

pointing parts out,

to their friends,

that they'd like to eat.

i can feel my skin, blistering.

under this heat.

must be reminding them,

maybe they can smell the pork.

the metal

cooking

me.

feels like it's cooking me.

whose fucking idea was this metal elephant.

the steel drums have been left behind,

they're back by the precinct somewhere

now it's music I've not heard before

sounds old fashioned.

a man is talking
he's saying some poem about spring.
the words don't make any sense
sounds like they're not in english
not in an english i know.
and no one is listening or looking,
at me,
they're all listening and looking at
him.

mark doesn't help me down.

is this it?

is it over?

    (She climbs down.)

nobody has told me what to do when it got to this bit.

and i make my way to the tree /

as i walk
the little kids mothers scoop them up into their arms,
tell them how well they did,
that they did great not to cry.
same babe

   / do you mind if she has a picture with you?
huh?

my little daughter. can she have a picture with you

it's the dad and his little girl

oh sure.

> *(She bends to the height of the little girl, smiles, it's big, fake.)*

thank you.

and he lifts her up

and says something like

come on angel

or

let's go princess

or

where next,

queen.

> *(She watches the dad and daughter walk away, music builds.)*

and i wanna tell him

i'm your queen today

i'm your queen.

but i don't.

i *don't* do that.

instead i just keep walking.

and walking

and walking

and

as i reach the wood

under the trees it's cool.

the temperature,

is perfect.

i find my one

his tree

the

oldest looking

the one with saggy bits

and knots in the wood

and sit down,

for a bit.

and wait.

BREATHE.

~~I know he's followed me,~~

~~of course he has.~~

~~one of them had to.~~

~~part of me is actually looking forward to it,~~

~~to move the story along.~~

hey

alright

he says

and he licks. his. lips.

did you follow me?

he says he didn't but obviously he did.

he says he likes my dress n that.

thanks

and that he saw me in the parade

oh.

he offers me a can.

and asks what I'm meant to be doing now?

what's next for a queen?

nothin, i just wanted to be by this tree.

it don't matter.

i was going back down now.

cheers for the can /

he asks why i don't stay up here a little bit longer.

i dunno

you can tell me about this tree he says.

and

he

comes

closer.

so.

i start talking about the fuckin tree

how it's meant to be what Cov was built around

and there's this whole thing about this guy called Coffa.

which is mad.

i know,

but i felt it.

maybe it's coz of the may queen thing,

maybe,

it's just a thing

that they wanted to do

to represent

like a ritual

and i thought i'd just come up here to find it

but i don't really know what i'm looking for

and as i'm talking

he starts

playing with the strap on my dress

and it's pretty clear he doesn't wanna hear about no tree,

so I

oh, uh, i can't get this dirty.

I /

maybe we should, go back down.

but he doesn't wanna go back down.
he wants to be right here with me, he says.
says he's been *waiting* for me.
his breath smells like sour apples and fags
and he's a bit
sticky
coza the heat.
but he's doing all the things
and saying all the things
that he thinks i want to hear
so i just sort of
let him do it.

it's quite easy.
you just turn your brain off
think of something else.
i've done it before
maaaaany times

i think about the elephant

and the tigers

and the popes and the nuns and the firemen

and the pigs

and how

milking the cow you must be

pure

virtuous

and maidenly.

***

I swear the moment he came he got a WhatsApp.

like a PING to signify the end.

and he

looked

at

his

phone.

as he was pulling out!

and he says he's gotta go.

whatthefuck?

and he's leaving

he is literally walking away

he's running away.

where are you going?

souuuund.

> *(Looks around. maybe drinks, maybe not,*
>
> *long*
>
> *uncomfortable,*
>
> *silence*
>
> *birdsong, natural, just like in a wood.)*

SHE ROOOOOOOOOOOOOOOAAAAAARS.

***

> *(Sounds of celebrations, getting louder.)*

I hear it before I see it

like a buzz

a hum.

and

down there

they look like they're

swarming

HOLY SHIIIIIIIIT

OH

MY /

I thought they were partying

it's hard to tell the difference

but this. THIS IS A RIOT.

like

actual

carnage.

cider cans being thrown

flags torn down then raised by hand

shouting

cheering

filming

Godiva gettin flipped from her horse.

her naked body

arching across the sky like some great renaissance painting.

people have started fires

you can smell um

it feels like the whole city is alight.

and there's spraying

and throwing

and chanting

or singing

i pick up a can

and go to look for my sister

n you know what?

people start to notice me

people start to notice <u>me</u>!

Like their queen has returned

and the chanting switched to

may queen

may queen

may queen

this is fucking brilliant.

the pigs have been let loose and are eating all the twelve pound burgers

the great elephant, stomping, taking out swarms of people,

and in the distance,

i see him running into the little supermarket on the corner

the man from behind the counter desperately tryna pull down his shutters

and so i swipe a stick that's leaning against a chair

them dancing men not needing it as much as me.

and i follow him in.

boys are just taking what they can

they get more cider

a massive bottle of vodka

fags

two of them cramming all these chocolate bars into their pocket.

But he, he is clever

just reeling off the scratch cards

stood on the counter

looking a bit like a young hero actually

a god

he smiles back at me

and the stick comes crashing down onto the counter

glass flies everywhere

feels

powerful

i keep going

hitting and smashing

and

take my weapon clean through the window.

but as i turn to him

ready,

    (She wields.)

the shutter guy runs in

screaming at me

not in english

but he gets so close to my face

so close that

yeh

it feels like he's threatening me

and then he looks down

just like he did earlier

that liiiiittle look,

and it catches him.

the stick.

right on the side of the cheek.

it's pretty amazin how quick the blood gets everywhere

red face

red neck

red chest

red hands

and i want to fly but i'm frozen

i want to get to the woods

to up there but i can't

i'm stuck

grounded

he's stumbled back into his counter

what's left of it

glass absolutely everywhere

and behind him I can see him running

again

running.

i go to run after him

someone pulls at the back of my dress

my peach dress

my sister is there

baby on her hip

why the fuck is the baby here?

screaming into my face

'what are you doing??'

what

are

you

doing?

and i look down

and there's a morris dancer's stick in my hand

my dress is red

and the man from behind the counter is on the floor

looking

scared as fuck,

actually.

not looking at me like he did earlier.

my sister grabs my arm to take me home

marches me through the streets like she's done a million times before.

we pass the partiers

and the revellers

and the people having, a nice time

a drunk time

but a nice one.

it looks

different.

> (Yanks her arm away from her sister's grasp.
> really looks. really looks around.)

it don't really look like a renaissance painting no more

it looks like

people

my people

having a party.

where are the rioters?

i say

what happened to the...

   'what are you on about?'

my sister snaps

it was all kicking off,

there was, people were

it was, carnage...

   a few kids started a fire and scared the fuckin horse.
   n they pushed that pole over.
   but you
   you have to take it too far don't you
   everyone's having a nice time and you just have to
   ruin it.

we keep walking

we keep walking when the police drive past us,

my sister dives in front of me to cover up my dress.

at home

I get in the shower

then,

She puts my dress in the wash

while i watch the baby fall asleep on her bed.

she comes in

and lies down next to me

what the fuck leigh?

tells me how pissed off mum is gonna be

and hugs me,

reeeeally tightly.

she used to do this all the time

before she had the baby

we'd always fall asleep together.

and when we was little she'd squeeze me so hard that I'd nearly stop breathing.

then i'd do it back to her.

we'd say it's coz we loved each other that much.

we'd say that if one of us ever stopped breathing,

when squeezing,

it's because we loved them more.

she doesn't hug me that tightly now

but i guess it's coz she's got someone else to squeeze that love into now.

i feel her breathing slow down

and she's asleep within minutes.

i'm not

i'm just here

waiting.

waiting for...

    (She knock knock knocks.)

the back of the police car is hot and sweaty and sticky.

and they act like i'm not there

laughing and joking.

taking the piss outta the people having a great time.

my people having a great time.

can you just pull over for a sec?

***

at the station

i see the bunch of lads

my sister was talking about

who've also been arrested.

an acknowledgment.

a well done

a

oh look they got her in.

it's herrr.

    that's good for you

    good for a girl

where is he?

i don't say anything to the officer

he's all stereotypes and cliches

and won't even tell me why i'm in.

makes remarks

not what a girl should do

not what a queen would do.

Last time I was here was on a school trip

genuine.

They used to take the year tens to Calais,

but now coz of brexit there's too much paperwork so we go to 'important places' in our city.

the police station is one of them.

fuuuucked it.

(She puts her hands over her face.

for a very

very

very

long moment.)

I'm gonna need an appropriate adult in a minute.

I'm not asking my mum so,

if one of you could do it that would be sound.

(She sits by or near someone.)

you don't have to do anything or say anything, jus sit there and be, appropriate.

He comes back in, thanks you for being here and asks me to 'acquaint him with what I've been up to this evening'

if you just say, in your own words, what happened
this will be a lot easier.

and he's off. like a train...

telling me they've got footage, and there are witnesses
that are happy to testify.

and an innocent man is in hospital,

he says they're enquiring about some youths and petty
theft and damages done to the local area,

but nothing of the same magnitude.

nothing compared it what I did.

and I wanna scream to him about Callum

and Jay

and Kofi

and the fireman

and my dad

and the dad

and him.

and what happened up the woods. with him.

and about the way *he* looked at *me*.

and about what mark said

and about the waiting

and about the tree

i've got this urge to tell him about coffa and the tree.

but maybe he'll think I'm lying

and

am I even remembering it right?

If there was no riot

and no looting

and it was just some kids taking it too far,

what was I making up?

what *bit* was I making up.

coz this is my story.

>   *is he gonna press charges?*

he says he doesn't know but I've got no previous so if it does go to court, he doesn't think they'll be too harsh on me. He just hopes this isn't a sign of things to come.

>   *it's such a shame. you looked so pretty in that dress. we all watched you, and then you go and do something like this.*

***

when i was little I'd always get really carried away with my imagination

like you know when you're playing make believe.

I'd get really involved.

I wouldn't know when to stop.

everyone else would just like, stop playing the game

it would fizzle out.

and I'd

keep

going.

even when we was having dinner

even when I'd wake up the next day.

I'd still be in that game.

kids get annoyed at shit like that.

so I'd just do it in my head.

and tell people these stories.

like the one about my dad being Orlando Bloom.

I used to say we had a pet tiger.

and I'd always say my mum was pregnant.

bless her.

forever getting asked at school when the baby was due.

must have been awks.

then i'd lie about how old i was.

how much i drank.

if i was a virgin.

where i'd been.

who i'd been with.

so when when it got to court,

which it did

he did press charges.

i wasn't sure what to tell them

i wasn't sure what was the truth.

***

Ashleigh Marie Jackson
24th feb 2005.

yeh

i don't know why i did it.

***

i can't go anywhere near the 'site of the incident', or him, or his family.

and i have to be home by seven each night,

I've also gotta do community service...

so obviously i'm watching _misfits_.

fingerscrossedforsuperpowers.

they made a show of me

it was more like a media thing. 'may queen beats up shop owner'

looked well good in the papers.

i even became sorta famous for a bit

but not in a good way

in a

i've pretty much been in bed ever since way.

i have to go to these meetings twice a week.

With a lady called Kay for _anger management_.

which is lols. coz i don't even feels that angry.

just, nothing.

she asks me to.

> _work on this helpful wee exercise for anger and anxiety,_

colours. in the room.

any colour

red

all the red things in the room.

find them.

go.

> (**LEIGH** *finds lots of red things that the audience are wearing. She isn't her chatty, witty self with the audience. she's just doing what needs to be done.)*

then she gets a bit deeper and asks where it's coming from. this aggression.

and i say

i dunno

she asks about my family

they're all sound

she asks about parents

my mum's cool n that.

nah don't see my dad.

she asks about relationships...

not really had one.

asks about men in my life.

i tell her i

don't really have any

i wanna tell her about my dad

but how do you tell someone about something that might be in your head?

and i wanna tell her about Coffa

but how do you tell someone about something that might be in your head?

and I wanna tell her about Callum and Kofi and, all of um.

but ~~how do you tell someone about something that might be in your head?~~

***

Coffa's Tree. Winter.

Just the setting of the tree in winter. bleak. bare. dead.

stark birdsong, sounds more eerie than in spring.

***

i used to think it were well fun growing up here. and like all my mates are all

around and you could go where you like and do what you like and it all felt like this whole

world in one little place. but now, i feel i don't even wanna go to the end of the road.

i just stay here.

i don't go to the shops

or the wood

or school

i just go to my classes with kay and come home.

my mum and sisters say they're worried about me

that i should start going out

even Sienna comes to the door but I ain't got nothing
to say to her.

But here in my garden i feel

feel safe.

stuck, but safe.

i sit in the garden a lot.

and watch the birds,

and wonder where they've been and where they'll go
to next

fuckin lucky buggers them,

doing what they want.

the robin is back,

and mum still says it's grandad,

but, you know, grandad wasn't aggressive like this little
shit.

he was gentle.

and this thing.

this, robin.

honestly

if anyone else tries to come into the garden,

it attacks um

like full on, flies at them.

and its song is so loud.

it proper doesn't give a shit.

we all think they're cute,

these robins,

but watching, i think they're lethal.

we're mates, me and him

i'm up as soon as it's up, and i watch out for it, most of
the day.

and one day, in march,

i feel like it really notices me,

it's all 'hey babe'

and i'm like

hey

and then,

i shit you not,

it lands. on the TABLE. and hops towards me.

these little jumps.

i stay proper still,

and it's maybe like *this* far away from me.

and it just stares,

for ages.

and it sings.

it's beautiful.

and then it fucks off.

i go in and tell my sister about it,

she says I need to get out,

i need to *talk* to *people*.

but i ain't go no one to talk to,

apart from...

                                   ***

Kay?

i know you think I'm angry
like you do all this shit to calm me down.
but...
what if there's a reason I did what I did?
an explanation.

    i'm open to anything you want to explain, Leigh.

ok great.
coz i think i did what i did because of like, tradition,
because i was the may Queen.

she's still smiling but she's got this little wrinkle
in-between her eyebrows which i'm reading as
whatthefuckleigh,

like, the whole thing was i was meant to be this May
Queen, this virgin, right? but; i ent a virgin.

in fact, i even did it right up by where i think the tree
was.

COFFA'S TREE.

i know it's mad.

i know.

but it keeps going round and round in my head and i can't stop the thoughts, and i do wonder if this

is why it all got so...why i hit him.

because the tradition was broken, because it wasn't carried out.

someone had to pay,

and it was him

and me. in my head i make up that it's the curse of Coffa

Coffa's got him

and spared me

coz it wasn't me that was the sacrifice

really

it was him.

because of what happened up the wood that afternoon was him

not me

i like to think his guilt has got to him

and maybe one he'll be found wondering the woods

begging

for forgiveness.

from me.

but really,

that this happened because I wasn't what Coffa wanted, what was <u>expected</u> at this tree.

she looks at me for aaaaages.

proper ages,

it gets a bit weird.

she's asks

    who told you all this?

Mark, the man from the council.

He said the whole reason Coventry exists is because of this old guy called Coffa, who had a tree, and that was what started Coventry. He made this place. And in olden times they'd take a young girl, as an offering up the woods, and, that's who i was meant to be.

pure

and virtuous

and /

she gets her phone out and I see on her screensaver

her

with a group of mates or sisters

and it feels weird that she exists outside of here,

outside of this room.

She googles

COVENTRY

scrolls down and clicks a link:

she shows me that Coventry wasn't built by a man called Coffa.

It was built around a Coven, which she tells me is a group of witches (or nuns)

and they added the word Tre, meaning settlement.

so

Coventry

pretty much

was a town full of women.

You see where this is going?

   That's all made up.

   there was no guy called Coffa.

   it's just a legend. a folk story. made up.

so i tell her

it's the winks

and the lip licking

and the practice kissing

and names

and the words

and the lack,

of words

and i tell her

the computer games

the punches

the crunches

the dms

the walking behind you
so close up behind you.

the stopping

the staring

jokes

picture sharing

picture taking

touching

just touching

really lightly touching

the crazy fuckin eyes

and i tell you it's

the actions they inherit

the actions you inherit

the reasons

and seasons

they do what they do.

but the robin was just doing what it needed to protect
itself

it wasn't a *bad* bird

it was doing what it had to do

to protect itself

like me. right.

that's all.

***

i decide on the day,

to the year,

would be a really good time to do it.

may day,

at the place where it happened.

it ent as hot as last year

it's just like,

nice

a perfect spring day. IT IS THE PERFECT SPRING
DAY.

i'm excited to Mark the occasion.

i take a bath,

as before.

i even put on my dress.

it's still got a slight brown mark on the front.

mum tried her hardest to get it out,

we bought everything you can,

Vanish

Dr Beckman's

the pink stuff

turns out bicarb, lemon and a bit of elbow grease is the thing.

that works the best.

i take a stick with me

not *the* stick

that got used as evidence

but a branch from the garden,

that *felt* right.

felt like it could do the right things.

one with sharp edges

and weight behind it.

and i've looked at how to cause maximum damage

which places on the body will rupture,

yield,

break,

most easily.

I walk,

out

on to Lapworth Road

right onto Hillmorton

heading towards,

oiiiiiiii

oh yeh

oiiii pretty girl

oh yeh him

i'm talking to you

yeh i know

you talking to me now?
i am blessed.

i could watch you walk all morning.

and I slip the stick in between the spokes on his bike,
and just like Godiva on her steed before him,
he flips
into the air
lands perfectly on the curb
and with the back wheel still spinning
some content from his head
falls out
into the road.

Sket.

Passing Sienna's house
she'll do it for me,
i just need to tell her what happened when we were ten
and she'll push her brother

out of the top window

clack

crack.

she tells me that i

     look really well

thanks babe!

     i still love that dress on you.

thanks. maybe you can come round later? for a squash or summin?

     yeh sounds good. happy you're feeling good babe.

A few doors down, there's a couple of boys playing computer games,

even this early

they are

shooting,

looting

and raping.

they love it.

they absolutely love doing it.

they're engrossed.

so when the wires from the very machine they love the most are tightened

round their throats,

they barely even notice

barely even look up.

as they slip into an eternity of games

it's just like virtual reality, really,

if you think about it.

Leaving theirs i pass the guys who,

once again,

are roasting the hog.

But they,

smell like pork,

as they slowly burn.

Their fires becoming too large for them to handle,

too large for the firemen to handle even.

a terrible tragedy.

It takes a while to walk to the council buildings

through the city

down highways

and round ring roads

and over cobbles

it's hot.

it's got hot

are you hot?

feels more like last year.

which is nice.

appropriate.

and when I arrive,

these buildings,

are even more impressive than last time.

everything seems,

bigger,

the nuns and the tigers and the

elephant

so big that I hitch my dress up,

and climb on,

Mark's office please.

I command.

Because an elephant is way more impressive than a
horse.

And everyone's looking at me,

so i smile and wave

and smile and wave.

until we reach

hello

it's meee

yeh i'm in the dress.

thank you.

it's a bit stained. but it's still my favourite thing to
wear.

we can make small talk about

birds

and how his job's going

and

how is it you came to decide that there should be a
virgin for this sacrifice, Mark?

and as he's talking in that really fucking annoying voice

and all i had to do was do exactly what i did before.

but mean it this time.

it isn't hard,

you just have to turn your brain off.

think of something else.

> *(She hits, just like with the morris stick*
> *before, ritual, dance.)*

it's pretty amazin how quick the blood gets everywhere

red face red chest

red wings

red hands

And i fly

i soar

up to the woods

i find the tree

the oldest with the knots and the saggy bits

and there's no one there

no Coffa

no Callum

no Orlandos.

they've all gone.

Just me.

Lightning Source UK Ltd.
Milton Keynes UK
UKHW020756210322
400370UK00007B/135